Bird Coloring Book 1

by RJ & IrisBenjamina
Photos by Chris R Johnson
Copyright 2019. All rights reserved.

Great Blue Heron

Wild Mitred Red-masked Parakeet

American Goldfinch

California Quail

Scrub Jay

Broad-tailed Hummingbird

Yellow-rumped Warbler

Anhinga

Tree Swallow

Cactus Wren

Turkey

Blue-grey Gnatcatcher

Scrub Jay

Yellow-throated Warbler

Yellow-rumped Warbler

Blue-grey Tanager

American Avocet

Wilson's Warbler

Blue-crowned Motmot

American Kestral

Acorn Woodpecker

California Quail

Hooded Oriole (male)

Black-headed Grosbeak

Greater Sage-Grouse

Yellow-billed Magpie

White-ringed Flycatcher

Yellow-bellied Sapsucker

White-crowned Sparrow

California Thrasher

Song Sparrow

Western Bluebird

Black-throated Blue Warbler

Western Bluebird

Yellow-rumped Warbler

Stripe-throated Hermit

Spotted Towhee

Hermit Thrush

Savannah Sparrow

Tropical Kingbird

Bay-breasted Warbler

Bananaquit

Western Meadowlark

Chestnut-mandibled Toucan

Yellow Warbler

Common Yellowthroat

Elegant Tern

Anna's Hummingbird

Golden Eagle

Long-eared Owl

www.ingramcontent.com/pod-product-compliance
Lightning Source LLC
Chambersburg PA
CBHW080229180526
45158CB00008BA/2306